Wiggle and Giggle

Movement Rhymes

Chosen by Kate Ruttle and Richard Brown
Illustrated by Alex Ayliffe

CAMBRIDGE
UNIVERSITY PRESS

Look at Me

by Michael Smith

Look, look, look at me.
I can stretch as tall as a tree.

Look, look, look at me.
I can fly like a bumblebee.
Bzz bzz bzz bzz
bzzzzzzzzzzzzzzz.

Look, look, look at you.
You can jump like a kangaroo.

Look, look, look and stare.
We can growl like a grizzly bear.
Grr grr grr grr
grrrrrrrrrrrrrrrrr.

Look, look, look at me.
I can jump just like a flea.

Look, look, look at Jill.
Let's copy her and *all stand still*.

Jump or Jiggle

by Evelyn Beyer

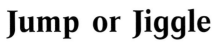

Frogs jump
Caterpillars hump

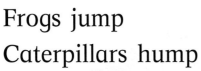

Worms wiggle
Bugs jiggle

Rabbits hop
Horses clop

Snakes slide
Seagulls glide

Mice creep
Deer leap

Puppies bounce
Kittens pounce

Lions stalk –
But –

I *walk*!

I Can Move
by Tony Mitton

I can move lightly,
light as a feather.

I can move
free as a leaf
blown by the weather.

I can reach right up
to tickle the sky.

I can curl tight
as an insect's eye.

I can spread out
in the shape of a star.

And I can *jump*!
Look how far . . .